See What You Can Be

Explore careers that could be for you!

by
Diane Heiman
and
Liz Suneby

illustrated by
Tracey Wood

This is called the copyright page of the book. If you look,
you'll find many careers right here.

The **editor**, Erin, was the first to read the manuscript. She helped the authors organize and revise their words, just as you revise stories and reports for school.

Chris, the **art director and designer**, worked with the illustrator and helped decide what to illustrate. She also selected the fonts, colors, and photos and put it all together on the computer.

Thank goodness, somebody checked the book for misspelled words and grammar mistakes. That was Judith, our **copy editor**!

Kendra and Gretchen, **graphic artists,** got the book files ready to go to the printer and made sure everything would print correctly.

As the **buyer**, Jeannette bought the paper and binding for this book. She made sure we had the best - quality materials for the best price.

Did you ever think of drawing as "work"? Being an **illustrator** is Tracey's job.

Mindy, a **production manager**, sent the files to the printer and watched while the book was being printed to make sure everything came out O.K.

Editorial Development: Erin Falligant

Art Direction & Design: Chris Lorette David

Production: Judith Lary

Kendra Schluter, Gretchen Krause

Jeannette Bailey, Mindy Rappe

Illustrations: Tracey Wood

Dear Reader,

You can and will be many things in your life. In fact, you already are! You're a daughter, a student, and a friend. Maybe you're also a soccer player, an origami master, or a musician.

When you grow up, **you will be many things**, too. You may be a mother, an aunt, and a volunteer in your community. You may also be an architect, a fashion designer, or a medical researcher. Can you imagine designing a solar-powered house or choosing the fabrics for your clothes?

This book will give you a **sneak peek** at the amazing things that women do every workday. You'll hear from women whose passions and talents have led them to careers they love. But, what do **you** love to do?

Read on to see where your interests might take you. **Try your hand** at some fun and facinating careers. Best of all, get ready to be inspired to dream about your future!

Your friends at American Girl

Table of

Contents

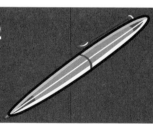

Personality Profile Bookmark

QUIZ
Which Careers Click with Your Personality?

To find out, check the **boxes** next to all the things that you like to do:

■ Play cat's cradle ■ Read a book in a comfy chair **■ Know what your present is before you open it** **■ Have a surprise party for your birthday** ■ Plant flowers **■ Play trivia games** ■ Play a team sport ■ Doodle in your notebook **■ Eat the same cereal most mornings** ■ Dance alone to your favorite song ■ Meet new people ■ Braid hair **■ Invent secret languages** **■ Play hide and seek—in the dark!** ■ Read your report to your class ■ Sing out loud when no one else is around **■ Discuss current events** **■ Read all the directions before you start a game** **■ Pull together new outfits from old clothes** ■ Put on your headphones to get lost in the music **■ Debate issues with teachers, parents, and friends** **■ Wear the same hairstyle most days** **■ Rearrange the things in your room** ■ Wash cars ■ Demonstrate dance moves ■ Spend time with one special friend

■ **Introduce friends from different parts of your life** ■ Mold clay into pots, animals, or beads ■ **Imagine life on another planet**

■ **Set your weekend plans in advance** ■ Do solo sports, like ice-skating or swimming ■ **Talk to people you've never met before**

■ Put on a skit with your neighbors ■ **Brainstorm ideas for new games** ■ Roll out cookie dough with your hands ■ **Follow a bedtime routine** ■ **Taste different foods at friends' houses**

■ Have friends over for a sleepover ■ **Learn your family history**

■ Keep a journal ■ **Know the weather forecast** ■ Build sand castles ■ **Explore new places** ■ Play charades ■ **Solve puzzles**

■ Play solitaire ■ **Take familiar walks** ■ Sing karaoke

Count the number of times you checked each color, and write the numbers in the spaces below:

■ **Purple**_____   ■ **Red** _____   ■ **Pink** _____

■ Orange_____   ■ Green _____   ■ Blue _____

Which four colors did you check the most?

The ways you spend your time and get things done are clues to careers that you might enjoy.

Green

You're a hands-on girl. You love being active or working with your hands.

Pink

You're a big thinker. You love challenging your brain.

Blue

You're a people person. You prefer to work with groups of people.

Orange

You're a true individual. You prefer to work alone or with a few others.

Purple

You're a shaker-upper. You thrive on constant change and new experiences.

Red

You're a straight shot. You thrive on routines and predictability.

Now you have your very own **personality profile.** Keep your eyes open for these symbols as you read on. If the symbols next to a career description match any of yours, check it out!

Turn to the back of the book to personalize a bookmark. Use it to save your spot as you explore the interesting things women do every workday.

If You Like
Animals

Name That Baby Animal

Sometimes a baby animal is called something completely different from the adult. Do you think the baby names below are correct? Check the answers to learn the names for some cute and cuddly, furry and feathery baby animals.

1. Kangaroo . . . . Joey   ■ True   ■ False

2. Turkey . . . . Chick   ■ True   ■ False

3. Whale . . . . Calf   ■ True   ■ False

4. Eagle . . . . Pip   ■ True   ■ False

5. Sheep . . . . Lamb   ■ True   ■ False

6. Cat . . . . Kitten   ■ True   ■ False

7. Goat. . . . . Kid   ■ True   ■ False

8. Toad. . . . . Worm   ■ True   ■ False

9. Dog . . . . Doggy   ■ True   ■ False

10. Horse. . . . . Foal   ■ True   ■ False

11. Swan . . . . Cygnet   ■ True   ■ False

12. Lion . . . . Colt   ■ True   ■ False

Animal lovers, turn the page to find out about the ways women work with creatures great and small.

Answers: 1. True 2. False (Poult) 3. True 4. False (Eaglet) 5. True 6. True 7. True 8. False (Tadpole) 9. False (Puppy) 10. True 11. True 12. False (Cub)

ANIMAL SHELTER CARETAKER

Personality matches:

What happens to lost or abandoned animals? Caretakers at animal shelters **feed, bathe, and play with them.** The best part of the job is also the hardest—finding good homes for the animals. Caretakers try to find each animal a happy home with a loving family or on a farm or nature preserve.

YOUR TURN

Find a pet a home

Have you outgrown one of your stuffed animals? Find her a new home by writing notes about what kind of animal she is, what her name is, what she likes, and the care she needs. See if you can find her a good home with a friend or sibling who will love and care for her just as you did.

DOG TRAINER

Dog trainers teach dogs to do all sorts of things, from obeying their owners to competing in shows to helping people with disabilities. Trainers **teach dogs to listen to human commands,** and they reward dogs when they do the right thing. Dogs are rewarded with affection, praise, and treats. Isn't that just what you want for a job well done?

YOUR TURN

Host a pet show

Invite your friends over to show off their favorite stuffed animals. Have each pet do a trick, such as sitting still or rolling over (with a little help, of course!). Make awards to hand out to the cutest, cuddliest, and most talented pets and their creative "trainers."

WILDLIFE PHOTOGRAPHER

Personality matches:

Flocks of geese flying south. Schools of salmon swimming upstream. Baby seals playing on the ice. Wildlife photographers **capture images of animals in their habitats** for books, magazines, posters, and the Web. Fun travel is part of the job, but so is braving bad weather, carrying heavy equipment, and working early in the morning and late at night.

YOUR TURN

Snap some super shots

What animals, insects, or birds do you see in your habitat? Grab a camera and head to your backyard or a neighborhood park. Point your camera behind a bush, under a rock, or up a tree. What do you see? Can you snap a shot before your subject flies or scampers away?

VETERINARIAN

Personality matches:

You know that veterinarians care for cats and dogs. Did you know that they also care for lambs, giraffes, and racehorses? Veterinarians **do routine checkups and make sick calls** for animals on farms, at zoos, and at racetracks. Whether animals are big or small, vets take care of them all.

YOUR TURN

Care for a virtual pet

Research how to care for the pet of your dreams. What should you feed your pet every day? How can you protect her from getting injured or sick? And best of all, what kinds of games could you play with your pet to keep her happy and healthy?

15

BEEKEEPER

Personality matches:

Beekeepers tend beehives and the bees inside. Beekeepers **carefully remove honey** from the hives without disturbing the bees. That takes patience—and protective clothing! The honey and beeswax that beekeepers harvest is used in products like candy and lip balm. Beekeepers also sell hives to farmers, because bees pollinate crops, which helps them grow.

YOUR TURN

Hunt down some honey

Who buys honey from beekeepers? Make a beeline for your kitchen cabinet and your bathroom counter to find out. Check the list of ingredients on food and cosmetic containers. Make a list of all the products you find that are made with honey or beeswax.

PET DETECTIVE

Personality matches:

Pet detectives are paid to help **find lost pets.** They gather information on the behavior of the lost animals, and they make posters and flyers to help spread the word. Detectives check local animal shelters for missing pets. And they track pawprints and use specially trained dogs that can follow a pet's scent.

YOUR TURN

Design a pet poster

Imagine you found a lost kitten. Create a poster to help find the owner. What would you need to have on the poster for the owner to know it's her cat? What information should you include to make sure the owner could get in touch with you? Where would you put the poster?

Meet a **Dog Trainer**

Martha Francis

Her very own Noah's Ark: Gerbils, hamsters, snakes, cats, and dogs . . . these are just some of the pets Martha had as a girl.

Teaching old dogs new tricks: Now Martha teaches classes for dogs, such as Puppy Kindergarten for pups and Tricks and Games for older dogs. She also teaches classes in obedience. Martha says that most dogs don't have good manners without good training.

Outside the classroom: Martha volunteers at an animal shelter to train dogs so that they have a better chance of being adopted. She also works with families and dogs on tough training issues.

Her trickiest training problem: One family called Martha because their dog didn't like to be left alone, and he bit anyone who left the house. The only time the dog wouldn't bite was if the person leaving was carrying out garbage, because he or she would usually be right back. What a dirty problem for Martha to fix!

Meet a **Wildlife Photographer**

photo: Mike Ostrander

Lynda Richardson

Inside the library: By age 9, Lynda was a regular at her local library. Eagles or beagles, slugs or bugs, lions or lemurs—if the subject was animals, Lynda loved to read about it.

Out in the field: Today Lynda takes photographs for the nature magazines she once read. How does she hunt down a great wildlife photo? Lynda researches animals to learn their habits and where they live. She also tags along with biologists who study animals in deserts, mountains, swamps, and forests.

Up on a cliff: Lynda says that wildlife photographers need skin as tough as an armadillo's. That's because taking photos in the wild can be quite an adventure! One night in Cuba, Lynda hiked up steep limestone cliffs to photograph hundreds of bats leaving a cave.

Back at the office: Lynda doesn't spend all of her time in the wild. She spends hours in her office, too, doing filing and billing. She also writes a monthly magazine column and gives lectures about photography.

MY ANIMAL JOURNAL

Would it be fun to be a(n)	Totally!	Could happen	Sort of	Not sure	No way!
Animal Shelter Caretaker					
Dog Trainer					
Wildlife Photographer					
Veterinarian					
Beekeeper					
Pet Detective					

Whoa!

Have any ideas, questions, or pet projects that will help you learn more about careers with animals? Write or draw them here.

Dogs at Work

People aren't the only ones with jobs. Dogs can be working professionals, too. Some specially trained dogs assist people who have physical disabilities. Other dogs protect sheep from wolves. Still others help police officers hunt down criminals. What a wonderful job it would be to teach dogs how to do their jobs!

If You Like

Food & Cooking

Take a Food Quiz

Think you might enjoy a career that focuses on food? Take this quick quiz to find out. You'll see that not all jobs in the food industry call for measuring cups and mixing bowls.

Yes **No**

☐ ☐ Do you like to try foods from different cultures and countries?

☐ ☐ Would you rather bake cupcakes for your birthday than buy them?

☐ ☐ Is going out to eat one of your favorite activities?

☐ ☐ Are you curious about what vitamins and minerals are in the foods you eat?

☐ ☐ Have you ever made up your own recipe for pasta, frozen treats, or a super salad?

☐ ☐ Would you like to pick your own fruits and vegetables from an orchard or garden?

☐ ☐ Do you like to shop with your parents at outdoor food markets?

Did you answer yes at least twice? Turn the page to find out which food-related professions you have "a taste" for, and try them out!

FOOD SCIENTIST

Personality matches:

Did you ever wonder who came up with the idea for yogurt tubes? What about fun-shaped fruit snacks? Food scientists **think up new ways to make and package foods.** They also inspect farms and food-processing plants to make sure they're clean and safe. That way, the food produced will be safe to eat, too.

YOUR TURN

Invent a squirt-proof package

Tired of getting squirted when you stick a straw into a juice box? Think up a better way to package juice. Draw a picture of your design, and add notes explaining how it works and what materials you'd use. Pull out your markers or colored pencils to make your package as colorful as it is clever!

CHEF

Personality matches:

Chefs love to cook, but they do much more than that. They plan menus and order all the ingredients, making sure they have enough food to serve hungry customers. Chefs manage the people who work in their kitchens, too. Last but not least, they **improve recipes and create new ones** to add to the menu.

YOUR TURN

Make up a new recipe

Take a favorite recipe and try three ways of making it even better. Add a drop of maple syrup to a smoothie or dried cranberries to a sandwich. Write up your favorite combo and give it a mouth-watering name, such as "Molly's Maple Dream."

ICE CREAM TESTER

Can you believe that people get paid to sample ice cream? An ice cream tester cuts cartons of ice cream in half to make sure ingredients, like fudge, are swirled evenly throughout. Tasters also **taste ice cream for flavor** using real gold spoons. Why gold? Because gold spoons don't create an aftertaste the way that wooden or plastic spoons do.

CHOCOLA

CHERRY

YOUR TURN

Host a taste test

Invite friends to test three brands of chocolate-chip cookies. Record what each tester says about the sensation of the first bite (crunchy or soft), the number of chocolate chips (too many, just right, or not enough), and which cookie he or she likes best overall. Which brand wins?

CAKE DECORATOR

Personality matches:

Cake decorators are artists. They **paint with frosting and use cake as their canvas.** Their beautiful and delicious masterpieces are served at weddings, birthdays, and other festive celebrations. A cake decorator needs a creative eye and a steady hand.

YOUR TURN

Decorate cute cakes

"Paint" cupcakes for your favorite holiday. Love the Fourth of July? Use red, white, and blue icing. Or try strawberries and blueberries for color. Add clever candy toppings, such as licorice whips for the stripes of the flag. How many designs can you think up?

FOOD SERVICE MANAGER

Personality matches:

Food service managers **feed hundreds or even thousands of people** every day! They work in places like hospitals, schools, and office buildings. Did you ever think about what it takes to run your school lunchroom? Food service managers order all the food, supplies, and equipment. They also hire, train, and supervise employees.

YOUR TURN

Plan a meal with your mom or dad

Help plan an entire dinner, from salad to dessert. Make a shopping list, and go along to the store to help pick out the food. Divide the grocery bill by the number of people in your family. What would you charge per person if you served this dinner in a cafeteria?

BAKERY/CAFÉ OWNER

Personality matches:

The owner of a bakery or café **runs a small business.** She finds a location, buys all the equipment and supplies, hires and manages employees, and creates and tests recipes. And that all happens before customers even walk through the door! Keeping customers happy is the most important part of her job.

YOUR TURN

Dream up desserts

What would you serve in a bakery of your own? Come up with a list of sweet treats, and write tempting descriptions that will make customers want to try them all—and come back for more!

Meet a **Food Scientist**

Chris DiPietro

What people think Chris does: Chris says that most people have no clue what she does. They think a job with "food" in the title means she works at a restaurant. She doesn't!

What she really does: Chris works at a spice company, where she is in charge of creating new products and making sure spices are pure and safe. She tastes and blends herbs and spices that come from all over the world.

How it all began: Chris first learned about spices when she was a little girl. Her grandparents were from Italy, and they made lots of tasty Italian meals. Chris loved math and science, too. Food science is the perfect "blend" of all of her interests.

The problems she solves: Chris tackles problems that most people don't even think about, such as coming up with ways to keep spices from sticking together in packets. Think of her the next time you sprinkle seasoning on your pasta or pizza!

Meet a **Bakery/Café Owner**

Judy Rosenberg

How her bakery began: Judy started out selling Valentine's Day cookies at local stores. The cookies were a hit. Soon after, Judy opened up "Rosie's Bakery." Who's Rosie? That's Judy herself! Her friends nicknamed her Rosie because of her last name.

The sweetest part of her job: Judy makes a living doing what she loves best—thinking up, dreaming about, and tasting desserts. She also works for herself, which means she can set her own hours. That gives her the flexibility to spend time with her family, too.

The stickiest part of her job: As a business owner, Judy has to buy supplies, pay employees, and set prices. She would rather spend her time making sweet treats, so she has a partner who helps with the financial part of the job. When it comes to business, Judy says that two heads are better than one.

Her favorite treats: Two of Judy's specialties are fudgy cookies called "Soho Globs" and brownies called "Boom Booms." Yum!

MY FOOD & COOKING JOURNAL

Would it be fun to be a(n)	Totally!	Could happen	Sort of	Not sure	No way!
Food Scientist					
Chef					
Ice Cream Tester					
Cake Decorator					
Food Service Manager					
Bakery/Café Owner					

Stir up the pot!

Have any ideas, questions, or recipes that will help you explore a career in food and cooking? Write or draw them here.

Mastering the Art of Fruit Tarts

Did you know that women go to school to learn how to become professional chefs? Cooking schools are called "culinary institutes," where you can even major in dessert. Imagine how fun—and delicious—your homework would be!

If You Like
Math &
Puzzles

Solve a Sudoku Puzzle

Can you fill in the missing numbers in this puzzle? Make sure every column, every row, and every box contains the numbers 1 through 6, but only one of each number.

Now flip through the chapter to see the many things women are doing with math and puzzles.

Solution:

6	2	3	4	5	1
5	4	1	6	3	2
4	6	2	5	1	3
3	1	5	2	6	4
2	3	6	1	4	5
1	5	4	3	2	6

AEROSPACE ENGINEER

Personality matches:

Aerospace engineers **design extraordinary machines,** from airplanes that weigh more than half a million pounds to spacecraft that travel over 17,000 miles per hour. The airplanes we travel on are designed by engineers. So are the planes used for defense and the vehicles used to explore space. An aerospace engineer's job is truly out of this world!

YOUR TURN

Design your own plane

Paper, of course! Invite a friend over to join you in making paper airplanes. Test out different designs and types of paper. Which plane flies farthest or fastest? Which flies the straightest course?

TRANSIT PLANNER

Personality matches:

Transit planners **map out routes for public subways, trains, boats, and buses.** They decide when and where transportation will stop to pick up travelers. To make those decisions, transit planners analyze lots of data, such as how many riders use each stop and which neighborhoods are growing or shrinking. Planners also listen to comments from riders themselves.

YOUR TURN

Map a journey

Map out a trip for your family. Go online and find the bus, train, or subway schedule for your town or the nearest city. Many Web sites have "trip planners" to make it easy for you. Find a museum, park, or other fun place you can visit without taking the family car.

CRYPTOGRAPHER

Personality matches:

Ancient Egyptians used cryptography to plot battles. They wrote secret messages using hieroglyphs. Today cryptographers **write secret codes to protect information** that travels over all sorts of networks, from PCs to cell phones to automated teller machines (ATMs). Cryptographers also work to break codes that other people have written.

YOUR TURN

Write in secret code

Mirror writing is a code that artist Leonardo da Vinci used in the 1400s. Now it's your turn! With a thick marker, write a message on a thin sheet of paper. Flip the sheet over, lay another sheet on top, and trace the backward letters onto that sheet. Hold it up to a mirror. Can you read the message?

ACCOUNTANT

Personality matches:

When you think "accountant," think money. An accountant helps **keep track of money** for another person or a company. Accountants set up *budgets*, or plans for how money should be saved or spent over time. The computer is an accountant's best friend.

YOUR TURN

Build a budget

How much money would you need to go to the movies with a friend? How much are the movie tickets? Would you buy popcorn and drinks for you both? Figure out the total cost, and the next time you go to the movies, see if you can stick to that budget.

REAL ESTATE DEVELOPER

Personality matches:

Do you have a favorite shopping mall? You can thank a real estate developer for building it. Real estate developers **buy land on which to build new offices, homes, and stores.** Sometimes they fix up old buildings that are already on the land they buy. Developers then rent out or sell those buildings to earn money.

YOUR TURN

Brainstorm a block of buildings

Think about the homes and businesses in your neighborhood. Choose a block of buildings that you would like to see replaced, and sketch out what you would turn it into. Do you wish there were a music store in your area? A rock-climbing gym? A Chinese restaurant? Develop it!

STOCK ANALYST

Personality matches:

One way to make money is to *invest*, or buy stock, in a company and hope it grows. Stock analysts **study businesses to see which ones may do well** in the future. Analysts then give advice to other people about which businesses to invest, or "buy stock," in. If a stock analyst is right and a business grows, investors can sell their stock to make money.

YOUR TURN

Choose a company with a bright future

Pick two stores or restaurants near your home that sell the same type of thing, such as pizza. Which restaurant has better food, service, and prices? Write a list of the pluses and minuses of each so that investors can decide which one to buy stock in.

Meet a **Transit Planner**

Elizabeth Gotterer

A journey begins: As a teen, Liz gladly took the bus from her home in the suburbs to her ballet lessons in downtown Baltimore. In college, she hopped on the subway to get all around New York City.

Stops along the way: When Liz moved to Seattle after college, how did she explore her new city? You guessed it—public transportation! Taking the bus was a great way to see the city and experience many different cultures and languages.

The trip continues: Now Liz designs routes for the buses she loves to ride in Seattle. She decides where the buses should go and how often they should pick up passengers. To make these decisions, Liz analyzes lots of information and listens to passengers themselves.

A wonderful ride: Liz believes public transit is good for people and the earth. It gives everyone—even people who don't have a car—the chance to travel. And fewer cars on the road reduces pollution, too.

Meet an **Aerospace Engineer**

Andrea Razzaghi

Winning moments: In school, Andrea always liked math more than reading or writing. Solving math problems was like winning a contest every single day.

It takes teamwork: Today, Andrea uses math to design and build spacecraft at NASA. She manages a team of engineers, who she says work like musicians in an orchestra—everyone brings special skills that make the group a success.

Out of this world: NASA engineers send satellites into space to look at Earth and report back about weather. They put telescopes into space to keep track of what is happening in the night sky. And they send spacecraft to explore other planets in our solar system.

Mistakes are A-OK: When Andrea was little, her dad encouraged her to try to fix things around the house. Andrea made a lot of mistakes, but she says that mistakes make you smarter—because you learn what doesn't work! Andrea and her team know that each mistake brings them closer to a solution.

MY MATH & PUZZLES JOURNAL

Would it be fun to be a(n)	Totally!	Could happen	Sort of	Not sure	No way!
Aerospace Engineer					
Transit Planner					
Cryptographer					
Accountant					
Real Estate Developer					
Stock Analyst					

Add it up!

Have any ideas, questions, or calculations that will help you learn more about careers in math and puzzles? Write or draw them here.

Girls Love Numbers

According to the National Science Foundation, more girls than boys have gone to college during the last ten years. And now, for the first time in history, more girls than boys in the U.S. are earning degrees in engineering. Those numbers add up to a bright future for girls.

If You Like
Sports & Fitness

Discover Your Sport Style

Would you rather play on a soccer team or cheer from the stands? Do you dream of meeting Olympic athletes or of winning your own Olympic gold? Follow this flow chart to your sports style.

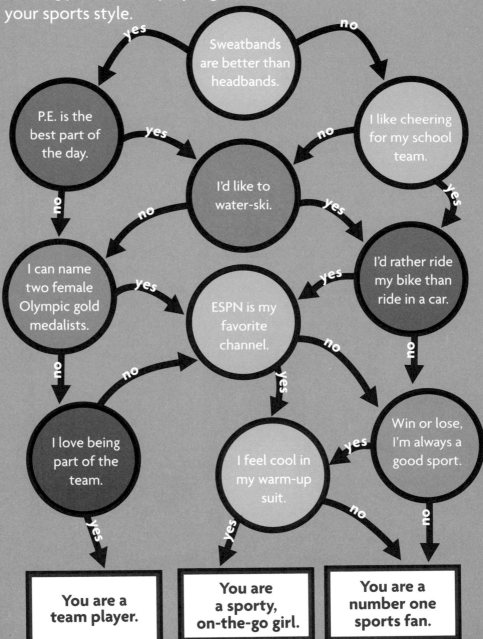

PHYSICAL THERAPIST

Personality matches:

Physical therapists **help people heal parts of their bodies** that are damaged because of injury or illness. They treat patients with exercise, stretching, and massage. Therapists also use machines that send electricity or heat to help the body heal. Finally, physical therapists teach patients to use crutches and other equipment that helps them do everyday things.

YOUR TURN

Work out a workout routine

Find a jump rope, a Hula Hoop®, and an exercise mat or towel for doing push-ups and sit-ups. Arrange your equipment in a big circle. Do some stretches, and then spend a few minutes at each workout "station." Take a quick breather in between stations. How many times can you go around the circle?

WHITE-WATER RAFTING GUIDE

Personality matches:

Here's a job where fresh air, sunlight, and booming rapids are your office! White-water rafting guides **lead people on adventure vacations.** They teach travelers how to stay safe while on the river, and they're in charge of the camping and cooking that happens along the riverbank each night.

YOUR TURN

Locate some raging rivers

There are many great rivers for white-water rafting across North America. Find the locations of these popular ones: Snake River, Ocoee River, Kennebec River, and Tuolumne River. Which would you like to navigate some day?

DANCE STUDIO OWNER

Personality matches:

Many dance studio owners were once professional dancers. They use their talents to **teach other dancers ballet, jazz, tap, hip-hop, and ballroom dancing moves.** Studio owners also have the responsibility of running a business, so they must be just as quick with numbers and money as they are on their feet.

YOUR TURN

Put on your dancing shoes

Look through your CDs, and choose a toe-tapping, get-up-and-boogie kind of song. Now *choreograph*, or make up a dance routine to go along with, the song. Practice by yourself in front of a mirror. Or teach a friend and practice together!

SPORTSCASTER

Personality matches:

Sportscasters **write and deliver news about sports** on the radio, TV, and Web. They interview athletes and give updates on sporting events. Sportscasters often report live from games, while the action is taking place. That means they don't get to practice their lines or redo their mistakes. They have to be ready for every curveball that comes their way!

YOUR TURN

Say it from the sidelines

Turn down the sound on your TV while you watch a tennis match, football game, or other sporting event. Pretend you are the sportscaster. Tell everyone what's going on during the event, using your voice to show your listeners just how exciting the sport can be.

SPORTS COACH

Sports coaches work with amateur and professional athletes, from middle-school players to national-league stars. Coaches **help their athletes develop skills,** endurance, and sportsmanship. They also look for talented new players and evaluate other teams to figure out how to play against them—and win!

YOUR TURN

Inspire girls to go the extra mile

Create your very own coach's handbook using a small notepad. Write the advice that you would give your team before a match or meet. What would you say after a thrilling win or a tough loss? Add a few cheers that you know will keep your players motivated.

STUNTWOMAN

Personality matches:

Stuntwomen are athletes and actors rolled into one. They **perform daring moves in movies and on TV,** standing in for the stars of the show. Stuntwomen do everything from jumping off rocky cliffs to racing cars and scuba diving. Many are trained as gymnasts, martial artists, rock climbers, or skiers before they get into show business.

YOUR TURN

Be a stunt double

Invite a friend over to be a stunt double. Make sure you both dress in jeans, sneakers, and the same color T-shirt. Take turns leading safe routines for the other to copy—anything from dance moves to tumbling. As "stunt girls," you'll have double the fun!

53

Meet a **Physical Therapist**

Pilar Rodriguez

A team player: Pilar has always loved sports, from track and soccer to figure skating and gymnastics—anything that gets her up and moving.

One false start: After college, Pilar took a job in an office, sitting at a desk. It didn't take her long to realize that she wanted to be more active at work. So Pilar went to school to learn *physical therapy*, or how to use exercise and massage to heal sore muscles, tendons, and joints.

A happy finish: Now Pilar is a physical therapist at a health club. She teaches people about fitness and helps them heal after injuries. Working at a health club means that Pilar can hang out with athletes like herself.

The ultimate goal: Pilar believes there's an athlete inside every person. Her goal is to bring that athlete out.

Meet a **White-Water Rafting Guide**

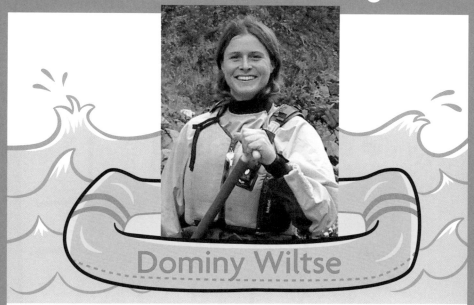

Dominy Wiltse

Working in the wilderness: Dominy leads white-water rafting tours in the beautiful wilderness of northern California. Every day she is surrounded by rushing rapids, ancient fir trees, and snow-capped mountains.

Watching the weather: Big rains or snowfalls affect the water level of rivers. The more water, the faster the rapids! Dominy keeps a close eye on the weather to make sure the trips she guides are safe and fun.

Practicing safety: Dominy says that orange life vests are a must on the rafts. If guests fall into the water, the vests keep them afloat until Dominy and other guides can pull them out with paddles.

Getting it together: Dominy has to be very organized. For over-night camping trips, she has a HUGE packing list—camping gear, food, water, and emergency supplies for every guest on the rafts. If Dominy forgets something, there's no turning back!

MY SPORTS & FITNESS JOURNAL

Would it be fun to be a(n)	Totally!	Could happen	Sort of	Not sure	No way!
Physical Therapist					
White-Water Rafting Guide					
Dance Studio Owner					
Sportscaster					
Sports Coach					
Stuntwoman					

Pump it up!

Have any ideas, questions, or statistics about careers in sports and fitness? Write or draw them here.

"You Go, Girls!"

That's what fans are shouting as they cheer for their favorite Women's National Basketball Association (WNBA) team. The WNBA is only about as old as you are, but millions of people in over 150 countries are sharing the excitement from the sidelines or by tuning in to national TV, Web casts, and radio.

If You Like

Art. & Music

Draw a Doodle Masterpiece

Your job is to turn each of these four doodles into a picture. Put pencil to paper and let your imagination lead the way. Whatever you draw will be a one-of-a-kind creation!

Read on to see how women express their creativity in the workplace every day.

FASHION DESIGNER

Personality matches:

Ever wonder who designed the clothes you love to wear? Fashion designers **create clothing and accessories** to keep us looking good from head to toe. They study style trends and then sketch their own ideas by hand or computer. Designers also pick out fabrics and colors, and they sew samples of their designs.

YOUR TURN

Fashion your own style file

Create a "wish book" of outfits that inspire you. Cut out pictures of clothing that you like from magazines and catalogues, and glue them into a notebook. Make separate sections for school clothes, party clothes, sport clothes, and chic accessories.

GRAPHIC DESIGNER

Personality matches:

Look all around you, and you'll see the work of graphic designers. They use computer software to design book and CD covers, menus, cereal boxes, catalogues, Web pages, store signs, logos, and much more. Graphic designers **pick images, typefaces, and colors** and then arrange them to grab our attention and communicate a message.

YOUR TURN

Design a new cover for an old book

You shouldn't judge a book by its cover, but you can design a new one for a favorite book. Find fun fonts and clip art on the computer, or draw your cover by hand. Make sure the title pops off the page, and add a drawing or photo that gives readers a hint about what's inside.

SONGWRITER

Personality matches:

Who wrote the words to your favorite song? It might not be the person you hear singing it! Songwriters **write the tunes or the words to songs,** and sometimes both. Most song-writers write songs for somebody else to sing. Every time a songwriter's tune is played, she earns money, which is called a *royalty*.

YOUR TURN

Put new words to a familiar tune

We all know the tune to "Happy Birthday." Now it's your turn to make up a new version with your own words. Try writing a snappy song called "Happy Summer," "Happy Snow Day," "Happy Weekend," or anything else that inspires you and makes you want to sing.

SOUND ENGINEER

Personality matches:

Do you like to download music, record music, or tinker with electronics? Sound engineers operate equipment such as amplifiers and speakers. They make sure that live bands and theater shows sound as good as possible. And they work in studios to **record sounds for CDs, TV, movies, and Web sites.** Does that career "sound" good to you?

YOUR TURN

Track TV-show sounds

When you watch a TV show, what do you hear *besides* people talking? Keep your ears open for music, the laughter of the crowd, doorbells ringing, and other sounds. Keep a running tally. How many sounds did you hear?

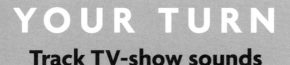

TV PRODUCER

Personality matches:

TV producers run the show! They make sure TV programs and movies **stay on schedule and on a budget.** Producers hire cast members and directors. They decide which programs and episodes are aired. They work behind the scenes, but without them, the show wouldn't go on.

YOUR TURN

Create a cast of characters

Choose a movie that you love. Write a list of the main characters, and then cast your family and friends in the roles. Who should your little brother be? Your mother? Your great-aunt? And how about you?

ARCHITECT

Personality matches:

Buckingham Palace, the Taj Mahal, the White House, and your house—architects were behind each of them! Architects **design homes and other buildings.** They draw by hand, use computer software, and make 3-D models of the buildings they design. Architects try to create buildings that look attractive but are also safe and affordable.

YOUR TURN

Brainstorm fantastic features

Pretend your parents hired an architect to redesign your home. You get to request some fun features. What will they be? A Tarzan swing in your room? A secret passage-way to the kitchen? A touch pad so that you can change the color of your walls to match your mood?

Meet a **Fashion Designer**

Kay Unger

A passion for fashion: Kay still has a note she wrote in elementary school that describes what she wanted to be when she grew up. She wanted to be either a figure skater, because she loved their fancy costumes, or a clothing designer, because she wanted to wear beautiful outfits.

The best birthday present: Kay received a sewing machine for her eighth birthday. She began making skirts and robes out of old quilts and towels. Sometimes she sewed by flashlight after bedtime.

Hard work pays off: Kay attended a school of design in New York City. She says she wasn't the most talented sketcher, but she was one of the hardest workers. In her opinion, success is 3 percent talent and 97 percent hard work.

A dream come true: Kay started a company to create clothes that would make women look and feel special. Now stores sell her elegant evening gowns, stylish dresses, and fashionable suits. Dreams do come true!

Meet a **Singer/Songwriter**

Scott Newton/ACL

Mary Chapin Carpenter

Songs at home: Mary Chapin needs peace and quiet to compose her songs. She pulls out her pad and pencil to write her lyrics and uses her guitar and a disc recorder to arrange and capture her tunes.

Songs on the road: In addition to writing songs, Mary Chapin performs her own. She has won five Grammys and sold over 12 million records. But giving concerts all over the world is exhausting. She is away from family and friends for months at a time. And before she found fame, she played in small clubs and earned very little money.

Songs can speak: Surprisingly, some performers, including Mary Chapin, are shy. As a quiet "tween" girl, she picked up her mom's guitar and taught herself chords. She practiced harmonies by singing along with records. Soon she found that writing songs was the best way to express her thoughts.

Songs from the heart: Mary Chapin often writes songs from her own experiences. She tries to keep her eyes and heart open to the world around her. She says that a part of her is in every song she writes.

MY ART & MUSIC JOURNAL

Would it be fun to be a(n)	Totally!	Could happen	Sort of	Not sure	No way!
Fashion Designer					
Graphic Designer					
Songwriter					
Sound Engineer					
TV Producer					
Architect					

Turn up the volume!

Have any ideas, questions, or doodles that will help you explore careers in art and music? Write or draw them here.

Beauty Through and Through

There is just one major museum in North America that displays artwork made only by women. If you take a trip to Washington, D.C., visit the National Museum of Women in the Arts. You'll find a collection of treasures—from Renaissance paintings to modern photos. Maybe your art will be displayed there one day!

If You Like
Computers

Learn Computer Lingo

Every profession has its own *lingo,* or special words and abbreviations. There is even lingo that girls can use when sending e-mails and instant messages. Do you "speak" this language? Draw a line between each abbreviation and its correct meaning.

LOL	be right back
BRB	are you O.K.?
ROFL	love ya lots
XLNT	laugh out loud
GTG	grin
GR8	great
SUP	talk to you later
RUOK	excellent
G	late for a date
TTYL	got to go
L84D8	what's up?
LYL	rolling on floor laughing

Thumb through the chapter to see how careers in computers can be GR8!

Answers: LOL (laugh out loud), BRB (be right back), ROFL (rolling on floor laughing), XLNT (excellent), GTG (got to go), GR8 (great), SUP (what's up?), RUOK (are you O.K.?), *G* (grin), TTYL (talk to you later), L84D8 (late for a date), LYL (love ya lots)

SOFTWARE ENGINEER

Personality matches:

Computers are only as smart as the instructions people write for them. These very detailed instructions are called computer *software*. Engineers **write, test, and update software programs.** But engineers don't write in English! They write in special computer-programming languages.

YOUR TURN

Invent a new software program

Did you know that until recently, you couldn't play a DVD or download photographs on a computer? What would you like your computer to do that it can't do now? Invent an idea for new software that will make your computer more helpful or powerful. Think big!

ANIMATOR

Personality matches:

What's your favorite animated movie or computer game? Ever wonder how it was created? Some animators draw by hand. Others use computer software to **create a series of pictures that look as if they are moving.**

YOUR TURN

Draw a cartoon character

An *inanimate object* is something that doesn't move or is not alive. Pick one, such as a backpack or a hairbrush, and turn it into a character for a movie. Give it a name, and sketch it doing its favorite activity.

COMPUTER SUPPORT SPECIALIST

Personality matches:

Many people rely on computers at work, so experts are needed to keep the equipment working properly. When monitors, keyboards, and printers break down, a computer support specialist comes to the rescue. These specialists **install computer hardware and software.** They fix and upgrade the equipment, too.

YOUR TURN

Share your skills

Do you know how to send an e-card or search for something on the Internet? Share your computer know-how with someone who needs it. Offer to teach a skill to a friend or family member, and lend support if he or she has questions later on.

TECHNICAL WRITER

Personality matches:

Technical writers **write instructions to help people learn to use computers and other equipment.** They describe technical information in a way that is easy to understand. Next time you get a new watch or computer game, you can thank a technical writer for the instructions that come with it.

YOUR TURN
Write it step by step
Practice writing detailed instructions just as a technical writer does. Capture every single thing you do to brush your teeth before bed. How many steps did you record?

HOW TO EMAIL
HOW TO PRINT
HOW TO PROGRAM
HOW TO START
HOW TO SHARE
HOW TO INSTRUCT
HOW TO SEND

WEB SITE DEVELOPER

Personality matches:

Web site developers create the text, images, sounds, and videos for Web sites. But that involves more than just making sites look fun and pretty. Developers have to **make sure the sites run smoothly,** too. Because of Web developers, you can shop, search for information, or play games on the Web.

YOUR TURN

Go on an online scavenger hunt

Go to americangirl.com to answer the following questions: Who is Coconut? Which cities have American Girl Places? What's on the cover of this month's *American Girl* magazine? Think about what features or games you would add if you were in charge of this site.

NETWORK TECHNICIAN

Personality matches:

Network technicians **connect computers and printers so that people can share information.** Technicians can set up networks within a home or an office. They can also create networks that connect people who live or work in separate places. The Internet is the largest network, connecting millions of people all over the world.

YOUR TURN
Make a yarn network

Stand in a circle with a few friends, and toss a ball of yarn from friend to friend. Hold on to the end of the yarn with one hand, and toss the ball with the other hand. When each of you has hold of a piece of yarn, give your piece a tug. Can everyone feel the tug? You've created a network!

Meet a **Software Engineer**

Ania Halliop

What can you do with math? That's what Ania asked a career counselor in high school. It wasn't until Ania took a computer-programming course in college that she found an answer. Programming is like math because both involve solving problems.

The first assignment: Ania had to figure out how to get a robot to take steps along a certain route. The instructions she wrote had to be detailed and accurate to make sure the robot ended up in the right place!

Telling computers what to do: Today Ania writes software that keeps information on computers safe when they are connected to the Internet. Ania's software makes it difficult for people to steal private information, such as bank account records. It also prevents people from sending viruses that corrupt computers.

Speaking lots of languages: Ania knows several computer languages. She also speaks Polish, since she was born in Poland. And she learned English when she immigrated to Canada as a girl.

Meet an **Animator**

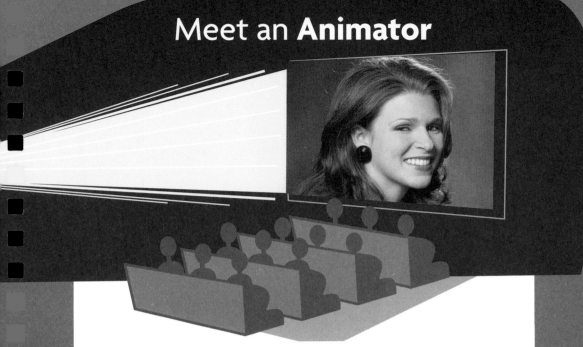

Elisabeth Franklin

Art from the start: Elisabeth hasn't stopped drawing since she first held a crayon at age two. But she didn't want to end up being a "starving artist." When her mom suggested she study computer animation in college, Elisabeth agreed. Hollywood—movies and money—sounded sensational!

Computers are her craft: Now Elisabeth works at a visual effects company in Los Angeles. She uses computer graphics to bring characters to life in movies, including *The Lion, the Witch and the Wardrobe*. Elisabeth says that computer animation is like posing a puppet, but you use a computer instead of your hands.

Big-screen excitement: Elisabeth's most exciting moment happened in a dark movie theater while she was munching on popcorn. *Scooby Doo Two: Monsters Unleashed* had just ended, and Elisabeth saw her name come up during the credits. She had made it onto the big screen!

MY COMPUTER JOURNAL

Would it be fun to be a(n)	Totally!	Could happen	Sort of	Not sure	No way!
Software Engineer					
Animator					
Computer Support Specialist					
Technical Writer					
Web Site Developer					
Network Technician					

Crack the code!

Have any ideas, questions, or Web sites that will help you learn more about careers in computers? Write or draw them here.

Big Ideas

Have you ever heard the word "entrepreneur"? An *entrepreneur* (pronounced on-truh-pruh-nur) is someone who has an idea for a business and then starts that business from scratch. The computer industry is filled with small businesses started by entrepreneurs. Do you have a good idea for a business?

If You Like

Reading & Writing

Pen a Poem

Think all poems rhyme? Think again! An acrostic poem starts with a word written down one side of a page. Each line of the poem begins with the letter on that line.

Here's an example:

POEM
Putting words
On paper
Enables me to keep
Memories alive

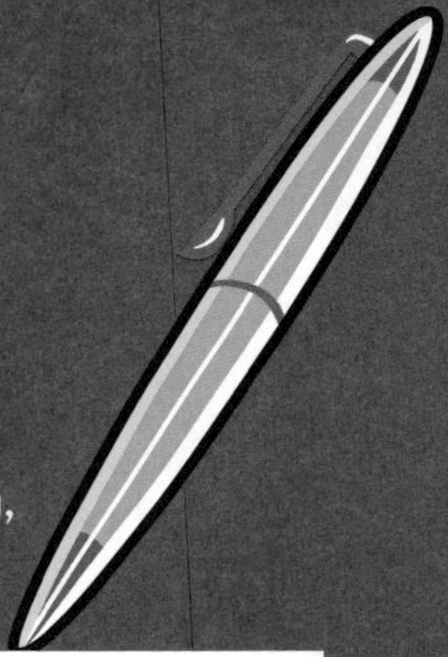

Now it's your turn. Pick any topic for your poem, from ice cream sundaes to chimpanzees.

After you finish your poem, read on about women who write wonderful words at work.

COPYWRITER

Personality matches:

Just do it.® This Nike slogan is an example of the powerful phrases that copywriters create to make products stand out. Copywriters create catchy names for products. They also **write advertisements and catalogue copy** that tell us why we should buy products. And the words on cereal boxes and shampoo bottles? Copywriters write those, too!

YOUR TURN

Name nail polishes

Pretend that you've been hired by a cosmetics company to name a new line of nail polish. Create a cute and clever name for each color of polish—from pretty pinks and purples to bold reds and blues.

SCREENWRITER

Personality matches:

Screenwriters think of ideas for television shows and movies and then **write all the words that the characters say.** Scripts for movies are called *screenplays*. Scripts for TV shows are called *teleplays*. Watch for screenwriters walking down the red carpet at the next Academy Awards.

YOUR TURN

Script a scene

Think up a movie scene about two sisters who want to convince their mom to let them get a pet. Write what each sister says to the other as they plot their super strategy. How does it all turn out?

NEWS JOURNALIST

Personality matches:

Journalists **research and write stories** about current events for newspapers, magazines, radio, TV, and the Internet. Some journalists report just the facts, and others share their opinions with readers. Journalists report on different topics called *beats*, such as crime, politics, fashion, and entertainment. Which beat would you choose?

YOUR TURN

Write a neighborhood newspaper

Publish a neighborhood newspaper with a couple of friends. Come up with a name for the paper, and assign stories for each person to write. Type up the stories, and make copies for your neighbors. Then wait for "Letters to the Editor" to come flying in!

CROSSWORD PUZZLE CONSTRUCTOR

Personality matches:

Do you have a clue how crossword puzzles are made? Crossword puzzle constructors use graph paper and computers to **create the connected words in crossword puzzles.** They sell their puzzles to newspapers and magazines. Sometimes they create puzzles for special occasions, such as birthdays and baby showers.

YOUR TURN

Create a crossword puzzle

Make a crossword puzzle out of your friends' names. Remember to number the squares that start each name, and write clues so that friends can figure out which names go where.

LAWYER

Personality matches:

There are many types of lawyers. Trial lawyers argue cases in court. Family lawyers give advice about things like adoption and divorce. Real estate lawyers help people buy and sell houses. All lawyers **make sure that laws are followed,** whether inside the courtroom or out.

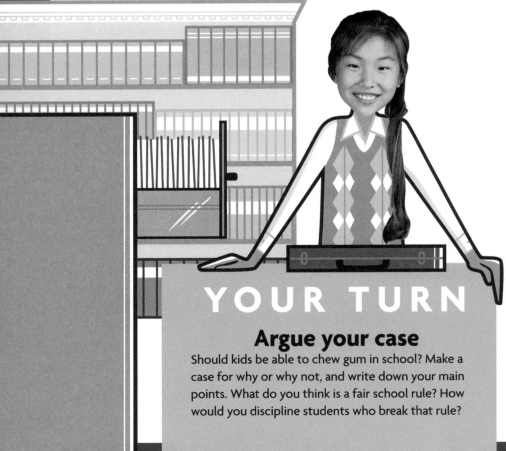

YOUR TURN

Argue your case

Should kids be able to chew gum in school? Make a case for why or why not, and write down your main points. What do you think is a fair school rule? How would you discipline students who break that rule?

DIALECT COACH

Personality matches:

People in different regions talk in different ways. You might be greeted by "Hi, y'all" in Alabama and "Hi, you guys" in Illinois. Dialect coaches help actors **learn accents, phrases, and words from different parts of the world.** Other times they help people lose their accents to sound more like the people around them.

YOUR TURN

Speak British English

Want to have tea with J.K. Rowling or the Queen of England? Then practice these British terms. When you crave cookies, ask for "biscuits, please." Need to borrow a sweater? Request a "jumper." And if your souvenirs don't fit in the backseat, ask to put them in the "boot," not the trunk.

Meet a **Screenwriter/Director**

Holly Goldberg Sloan

Once upon a time: Holly has always loved telling stories, and people have always loved listening to them. When she was a child, her mother would ask her and her brothers, "What happened at school today?" Her brothers would reply, "Nothing." But not Holly. She would tell one story after another.

An A+ in storytelling: Holly's second-grade teacher knew Holly had a knack for storytelling and wrote in her report card, "I hope for the rest of her life Holly continues to write stories." Thankfully, she has!

From scenes to scenery: Now Holly uses her storytelling skills to write and direct movies. Her creativity doesn't end with words. As a director, she also makes creative decisions about costumes and scenery. Have you seen the movie *Angels in the Outfield*? Guess who wrote it?

Meet a **Copywriter**

Kate Zartler

A way with words: Putting pen to paper has always come naturally to Kate. She thought about becoming a poet but worried that she wouldn't earn enough money. Instead, she tried her hand at advertising. Kate says that writing ads is like writing poetry because you have to express ideas with just a few powerful words.

Wherever words are found: Kate writes words for fast-food packaging and for magazine, radio, and TV advertisements—anywhere people learn about products. In fact, she was part of the team that wrote the words on McDonald's first "Happy Meal" box!

Keeping up with what's cool: Kate needs to be up on the latest trends. She says New York City is the ideal place for her to live because she spots trends even before they appear in movies and magazines.

MY READING & WRITING JOURNAL

Would it be fun to be a(n)	Totally!	Could happen	Sort of	Not sure	No way!
Copywriter					
Screenwriter					
Journalist					
Crossword Puzzle Constructor					
Lawyer					
Dialect Coach					

Write on!

Have any ideas, questions, or words of wisdom about careers in reading and writing? Write or draw them here.

A Powerful Poem

In 1893, teacher and writer Katharine Bates climbed Pikes Peak in Colorado. When she reached the top, Katharine was breathless—not from the hike, but from the spectacular view! The sight inspired her to write the poem "America the Beautiful." Now, over 100 years later, the poem lives on in the form of a song. Do you know the words?

If You Like
Science & Nature

Pick Your Perfect Place

Scientists and naturalists work in many environments to learn about the world. Where might they find you?

1. **Would you rather sleep**
   - ☐ **a.** under the stars or
   - ☐ **b.** in a warm log cabin?

2. **Would you rather see jellyfish while**
   - ☐ **a.** wading in a tide pool or
   - ☐ **b.** visiting an aquarium?

3. **Would you rather gather a beautiful bouquet from**
   - ☐ **a.** a garden or
   - ☐ **b.** a flower shop?

4. **Would you rather watch the rain fall**
   - ☐ **a.** from under an umbrella or
   - ☐ **b.** from a cozy window seat?

5. **Would you rather**
   - ☐ **a.** go apple-picking or
   - ☐ **b.** bake apple pie?

6. **Would you rather cook s'mores**
   - ☐ **a.** at a campfire or
   - ☐ **b.** in the kitchen?

7. **Would you rather look at animal tracks**
   - ☐ **a.** out in the woods or
   - ☐ **b.** on a fossil under a microscope?

How did you score?

Mostly a's: You're in your element outside in the fresh air.

Mostly b's: You're snug as a bug in a rug indoors.

Read on to discover how women are exploring the wonders of science and nature, indoors and out.

PALEONTOLOGIST

Personality matches:

Paleontologists are scientists who **study prehistoric fossils.** They travel to different sites to find the fossils, which are formed in mud and sand left behind from the days of dinosaurs. In a lab, paleontologists examine fossils under microscopes. What they see gives them—and us—lots of information about the history of life on Earth.

YOUR TURN

Create a time capsule

Someday people will consider your lifetime ancient history. Create a time capsule—a collection of things that show how life is today. Include items such as your report card, a wrapper from a candy bar, and a page from the newspaper. Save your time capsule to open again in ten years, or even twenty!

ORGANIC FARMER

Personality matches:

Organic farmers **grow crops and raise animals using earth-friendly alternatives to chemicals.** All farmers try to help their crops grow and protect them from diseases, weeds, and pests. But organic farmers use a natural approach. They use insects such as ladybugs to eat pests, and they fertilize crops using decayed plants and animal waste.

YOUR TURN

Try out your green thumb

Some plants can be grown from food in your kitchen. Nibble on a full-sized carrot until only two inches are left at the top. Place the carrot top in a pie pan with pebbles and water. Keep the carrot watered and in a sunny spot. Now watch for those greens to sprout!

OUTDOOR NATURALIST

Personality matches:

This is a job for women who like to get their hands dirty! A naturalist **studies and teaches others about the outdoors.** She may teach people how to track animals, how to build fires, or how to safely climb rocks and steep trails. Naturalists have a deep appreciation for our environment, and they share it by teaching others what they know.

YOUR TURN

Make leaf rubbings

Go outside and collect several leaves of different shapes. Place a sheet of paper on top of the leaves, and rub over them with a crayon or the side of a pencil point. If you can't find leaves, place the paper against a tree trunk and create a rubbing of the bark beneath.

MEDICAL RESEARCHER

Personality matches:

When you think of doctors, you probably think about the ones who help sick patients at clinics and hospitals. But many doctors work behind the scenes in laboratories. Medical scientists **research cures for human diseases.** They also find ways to prevent illness, such as by proving the link between smoking and lung cancer.

YOUR TURN

Keep germs away

Hand-washing is one of the most effective ways to keep germs from spreading. Find five ways to remind your family to wash their hands. How about posting little notes on mirrors or tissue boxes? Or putting out a basket of fluffy hand towels and colorful soaps?

ELECTRICIAN

Personality matches:

Without electricity, you couldn't watch television, pop popcorn in the microwave, or play on the computer. Electricians **set up and repair electrical systems.** They carefully follow written plans, called *blueprints*, to put wiring behind walls, floors, and ceilings. Then they test the wiring to make sure the system is working safely.

YOUR TURN

Make static electricity

Have you ever walked across the rug, reached for the doorknob, and—ouch!—gotten a shock? That's static electricity. To create electricity, blow up a balloon, rub it against your pants, and hold it against the wall. Does the balloon stick? That's static electricity, too!

STORM WATCHER

Personality matches:

Storm watchers are meteorologists who **study severe weather, such as tornados, tsunamis, and hurricanes.** Sometimes storm watchers work right in the middle of the storm, collecting information about wind speed and air temperature. Often they work at the computer studying past storms. Their findings help keep people and property safer from Mother Nature's wrath!

YOUR TURN

Name the hurricanes

Name next year's tropical storms and hurricanes the way that meteorologists do. Choose names alphabetically, alternating between girls' and boys' names. Can't think of a name that starts with U? That's O.K.—the professionals skip the letters Q, U, X, Y, and Z, so you can, too!

Meet a **Paleontologist**

Eva Koppelhus

A "paleo" what? *Paleontologists* are scientists who study dinosaur bones and prehistoric plants. Eva specializes in plants, something she's loved since she was a little girl in Denmark. While she rode with her father through the countryside, she tried to name all the plants she saw around her.

Under a microscope: Eva collects samples of rocks formed from mud and sand deposited during the time of the dinosaurs. Back at her lab, she studies these samples under a powerful microscope. She looks for teeny-tiny fossils of plant pollens and spores. Some of the pollen grains are still perfectly formed, even after millions of years.

Playing detective: Eva compares her findings to what other scientists have found to see how plants have changed over time. For instance, did you know that ferns are ancient plants far older than dinosaurs? But, unlike dinosaurs, ferns are still thriving on earth today.

Meet an **Organic Farmer**

Emeline Crawford

Food from the earth: Corn, parsley, green beans, squash, tomatoes, and onions—these are just some of the 40 organic vegetables and herbs that Emeline Crawford, nicknamed "Moie," grows on her New Morning Farm in rural Pennsylvania.

Hard work helps the harvest: Growing vegetables requires lots of hands-on work, but Moie is up to the challenge. She has always liked physical work. When she was a young woman, she painted walls and did construction work.

To market, to market: Every Sunday, Moie drives 125 miles to Washington, D.C., to sell her produce at an outdoor market. She also sells her farm's bounty to restaurants and stores.

Sunshine makes her smile: Farm work, like every job, has stressful moments. Moie worries about bad weather, vegetables ripening too quickly, and animals eating her plants. But focusing on the beauty of the farm around her brings Moie peace.

MY SCIENCE & NATURE JOURNAL

Would it be fun to be a(n)	Totally!	Could happen	Sort of	Not sure	No way!
Paleontologist					
Organic Farmer					
Outdoor Naturalist					
Medical Researcher					
Electrician					
Storm Watcher					

Explore galore!

Have any ideas, questions, or experiments that will help you investigate careers in science and nature? Write or draw them here.

You Passed!

Did you know you took a test on the day you were born? One minute after your birth, a doctor or midwife rated your health on a scale of 1 to 10 using a test called the Apgar score. Dr. Virginia Apgar developed the test in the 1950s. She was one of the first female doctors and was the first woman to become a full professor at Columbia University.

A World of Possibilities

You've just read about a few of the oh-so-many careers women enjoy. Here's a list of many more to help you imagine your own bright future:

Sign Language Interpreter • **Mystery Shopper** • Investment Banker • Information Technology Manager • **Toy Designer** • **Teacher** • **Perfume Tester** • **Product Manager** • **Color Consultant** • **Cartographer** • **Camp Director** • **Choreographer** • Comedian • **Nutritionist** • Blog Editor • **Trend Spotter** • **Event Planner** • Pilot • **Army Sergeant** • Nurse • **Yoga Instructor** • **Phlebotomist (you'll have to look this one up!)** • **Botanist** • Plumber • Security Analyst • Llama Breeder • **Florist** • **Snow Safety Patroller** • **Postal Service Worker** • **Quality Control Manager** • Customer Service Representative • **Judge** • **Insurance Agent** • **Milliner** • **Geologist** • Greeting Card Writer • **Flight Attendant** • **Real Estate Broker** • **Venture Capitalist** • **Hairstylist** • **Automobile Designer** • Actress • **Marketing Communications Manager** • Mechanic • **Maple Syrup Maker** • Marlin Fisher • **Literary Agent** • **Physicist** • **Police Officer** • Publicist • **Diplomat** • **Jeweler** • **Loan Officer** • **Auctioneer** • Acupuncturist • **Machinist** • **Makeup Artist** • Roller Coaster Designer • **Psychiatrist** • **Acting Coach** • Retail Buyer

• Professional Organizer • Minister • Rabbi • **Costume Designer** • Market Researcher • **State Trooper** • **Innkeeper** • **Masseuse** • **Financial Planner** • **Fund-Raiser** • **Pollster** • Social Worker • Heating & Air Conditioning Contractor •

Politician • **Landscape Architect** • Environmental Engineer • **Butcher** • Baker • **Candlestick Maker** • Woodworker • **Search and Rescue Captain** •

Human Resources Manager • **Historic Preservationist** • **Translator** • Private Detective • Interior Designer • **Town Manager** • **X-Ray Technician** • **Tour Guide** • **National Park Ranger** • **House Painter** • **Surgeon** • **Custodian** •

Librarian • **Poet** • **Fire Fighter** • Court Stenographer • **Chiropractor** • **Professor** • Museum Curator • Piano Tuner • **School Principal** • Jockey • **Pharmacist** • **Newscaster** • **Optometrist** • Ophthalmologist • **Air Traffic Controller** • Bandleader • **Concierge**

• **CTO (Chief Technology Officer)** • **CFO (Chief Financial Officer)** • **CLO (Chief Legal Officer)** • CPO (Chief People Officer) • **CMO (Chief Marketing Officer)** • **CEO (Chief Executive Officer—the big boss!)**

Write to us!

What do you love to do? What do you hope to become? Tell us about the careers you're interested in and how you're learning more about them.

Send letters to:
See What You Can Be Editor
American Girl
8400 Fairway Place
Middleton, WI 53562

(All comments and suggestions received by American Girl may be used without compensation or acknowledgment. Sorry—photos can't be returned.)

See What You Can Be

My Personality Profile

☐ **Hands On**

☐ **Big Thinker**

☐ **People Person**

☐ **True Individual**

☐ **Shaker-Upper**

☐ **Straight Shot**

Tear off this bookmark and check your four highest scores from the Personality Profile Quiz on pages 6 and 7.

Sign Language Interpreter • Automobile Designer • Investment Banker • Information Technology Manager • Toy Designer • Teacher • Perfume Tester • Product Manager • Color Consultant • Cartographer • Camp Director • Choreographer • Comedian • Nutritionist • Blog Editor • Trend Spotter • Event Planner • Pilot • Army Sergeant • Nurse • Yoga Instructor • Phlebotomist (you'll have to look this one up!) • Botanist • Plumber • Security Analyst • Llama Breeder • Florist • Snow Safety Patroller • Postal Service Worker • Quality Control Manager • Customer Service Representative • Judge • Insurance Agent • Milliner • Geologist • Greeting Card Writer • Flight Attendant • Real Estate Broker • Venture Capitalist • Hairstylist • Mystery Shopper • Actress • Marketing Communications Manager • Mechanic • Maple Syrup Maker • Marlin Fisher • Literary Agent • Physicist • Police Officer • Publicist • Diplomat • Jeweler • Loan Officer • Auctioneer • Acupuncturist • Machinist • Makeup Artist • Roller Coaster Designer • Psychiatrist • Acting Coach • Retail Buyer • Professional Organizer • Minister • Rabbi • Costume Designer • Market Researcher • State Trooper • Innkeeper • Masseuse • Financial Planner • Fund Raiser • Pollster • Social Worker • Heating & Air Conditioning Contractor • Politician • Landscape Architect • Environmental Engineer • Butcher • Baker • Candlestick Maker • Woodworker • Search and Rescue Captain • Human Resources Manager • Historic Preservationist • Translator • Private Detective • Interior Designer • Town Manager • Tour Guide • National Park Ranger • House Painter • Surgeon • Custodian • Librarian • Poet • Fire Fighter • Court Stenographer • Chiropractor • Professor • Museum Curator • Piano Tuner • School Principal • Jockey • Pharmacist • Newscaster • Optometrist • Opthamologist • Air Traffic Controller • Band Leader • Concierge • CTO (Chief Technology Officer) • CFO (Chief Financial Officer) • CLO (Chief Legal Officer) • CPO (Chief People Officer) • CMO (Chief Marketing Officer) • CEO (Chief Executive Officer—the big boss!)